Only In America:

From Hot Coffee To Scrambled Eggs To Nuclear Submarines

Robert Crosby

Publishing Layout by Michelle McClain Jackson
Cover Design by AJM Consulting
Copyright © 2016 Robert Crosby

Disclaimer:
The words in this book are provided based on the personal experiences of Rob Crosby and are meant to inspire others to use a positive Attitude and a Strong Work Ethic to achieve their dreams. Nothing written herein constitutes endorsement by the Department of the Navy.

For additional information, please go to www.boostachild.com

ISBN:1539773116
ISBN-13:9781539773115

Contents

Foreword

As I sat unenthusiastically in the waiting room of the oncologist office, I noticed a middle-aged gentleman approaching the nurse's station. While he waited in line to check in, I heard him paying compliments to everyone he encountered. They were total strangers but his radiance and energy permeated the room and brought smiles and laughter to all those around him. Watching his engagement with the staff, I wondered what his secret sauce was to happiness.

After he signed in, I watched him from the corner of my eyes as he floated past numerous empty seats, only to sit in a chair right next to me. He looked familiar. I recalled first meeting him at the Secretary of Navy All Hands meeting at the Naval War College. A few months had passed since I last spoke to LCDR Crosby and here we were, sitting in the waiting room.

When I entered the waiting room, I chose a seat in the far corner of the large room hoping not to see or talk to anyone. I was emotionally consumed in self-pity and I didn't need any additional distractions. I knew my path to healing was going to be a long and encumbered road plagued with chemotherapy and radiation and multiple surgeries in between. I was otherwise a very healthy person with no family history of cancer. Life had dealt me a bad hand and like the phenomenal poker player I am, I needed to play the hand I was dealt. But for now, the only thing I wanted was revenge on cancer for wreaking havoc on my life. How unfair life was. I couldn't shake the fear of dying; my emotions took over and I became anxious and angry. My parents have always taught me that when faced with something that puts you in a negative mood never relinquish the power to the enemy; always maintain your awareness and fortitude to change your focus to get yourself out of that mindset. I knew better but convinced myself that this situation was different so without protest, I kept my bad attitude. I expected my attitude to make me feel better, but just like dad said, it never does.

As I sat with LCDR Crosby, I was reluctant to talk about my situation. Rob shared his story which touched my soul and inspired me to find the motivation and determination to stay strong, keep the faith, and never surrender to the enemy. It was only 3 weeks since I was diagnosed and already, I was tired. Being angry was exhaustive and the time had come to expunge self-pity and grief and embrace faith and patience. If I were going to survive this, I needed to let go and let God take control. Our discussion was brief but the impact has forever reshaped my thinking and changed my life. LCDR Crosby told me about his journey from Hot Coffee to Nuclear Submarines, giving thanks to God and the many servant leaders that helped him along the way. His story was astounding and inspired hope and strength. To have grown up in the poorest region of the country - the Mississippi Delta - and be promoted from an enlisted Cook to now, a Nuclear Submarine Officer in the Navy was a true testament to his determination, work ethic and attitude. He reminded me that bad things sometimes happen to good people, but with the right attitude, you can make the most of what God has given you. It was definitely God's plan for us to cross paths that day and now our families will be divinely linked forever.

"CDR Jackson", the nurse called, "the doctor is ready to see you". I bid farewell to Robert and thanked him for his encouragement. I followed the nurse down a long corridor passed many offices. I remember peering into an open office door and getting a glimpse of a plaque on the wall. It read, "A bad attitude is like a flat tire, you can't go anywhere unless you change it". I got goose bumps and then smiled; it was confirmation that our meeting was not an accident.

Only in America inspires people of all ages, and gives hope to those facing hardships to never give up. LCDR Crosby emphasizes the **Power** in **Thinking Positively** and maintaining a great attitude and a strong work ethic. By doing so, you don't have to continue living in neutral. Once I stopped allowing cancer to take control, I came to accept that my experience was not just about me. My situation was an opportunity for growth and through God's grace and mercy, I too could use my experience to benefit others.

Thank you Rob for your attitude of gratitude and sharing your secrets to happiness and success. I share your sentiments that we were all born to win, but to be a winner, it starts with Y-O-U.

Today my friend,
I Salute YOU, for all that you have poured into my life.
I Salute YOU, for your prayers of strength and words of encouragement.
I Salute YOU, for having a great attitude and always seeking the best in every situation.
I Salute YOU, for having the courage and obedience to use your talents for God's plan.
I Salute YOU for taking action to change the world, and to inspire people through your story.
America, your destiny is calling. It's time to empty out the negatives and sprinkle a little AWE {Attitude & Work Ethic} in your life.

CDR Michelle McClain Jackson, HR
USN

x

Dedication

The sole purpose of this book is to encourage others by tapping into their endowed gifts of a positive Attitude and a strong Work Ethic (A&W). If properly utilized and cherished, one will be in AWE of how others will go to great lengths to assist professionally or personally. I would like to thank so many for assistance in creating this book. To name them all would certainly take up the length of the entire piece:

Dr. Bundy: Your mentorship and guidance are like arrows in the hands of a warrior. If I inspire ¼ of the folks you have encouraged, my life's work would be nearly complete. Thank you for genuine mentorship, friendship, and showing when you want something, the entire universe conspires in helping you to achieve it.

Family

My wife-Debra: Subway 1995, you walked in to order a "Seafood and Crab" sandwich, I flirted, walked it to your car, and was fired...but came away with you. You loved that 21 year old, Mississippi country boy's faults and idiosyncrasies, and visualized his potential. Thank you for never changing.

To my first born-Robert: At the tender age of 18, you were hand delivered by God to me. The burning desire to be a great father to you, ignited my love to serve this wonderful nation.

To my second born-Adreana: My only daughter. Your smile and encouragement light my universe.

To my third born-Zachary: My ambassador and God's angel of peace. Easy to raise and love.

To my twins-Julian and Jaxon: Two to wash, Two to dry, Two to fight, Two to cry, but most important Two to love. You are Proof of God's double portion of blessings on my life.

To my BOOST partners: Nicole Nelson, Michelle McClain-Jackson, Marty Conner, Adreana Crosby and Shenetta Darby.

Let's change the World together.

Chapter 1
A Mothers Love

A mothers love, a gift from God, a special gift that God puts into all Moms, a gift to love their kids and protect them even if it meant putting their own life at risk to make sure that there is no danger against their children.

I was born in a small town called Hot Coffee, Mississippi. My father had five children by five different women; some of these children were older than my mother. My father, a hustler, was abusive. My mother would escape my father's abuse by visiting my grandparents' house to do laundry. One day, she decided to stay permanently. My mother, who had only an eighth grade education, was now alone with three children. Still, she knew it was more important to protect her children than to stay in an abusive relationship.

Chapter 2
Spring

You can cut all the flowers, refuse to plant and nurture more seeds, but you cannot keep Spring from coming.

After living with my grandparents for a while, my mother was offered a place to stay with my aunt in the Mississippi Delta, the poorest district in the poorest state in America. It was during this time that my mother remarried. WJ, my step father, provided a source of financial stability for us. Soon after, my other two siblings were born. WJ now had a wife and five children to care for on a salary of $150/week. We were extremely poor. We did not own a car. I wore my sister's shoes to school, and WJ walked five miles to work every day. Because we were so poor, I was often bullied at school. Unfortunately, my parents' relationship began to sour as domestic violence again reared its ugly head. My life consisted of a continual cycle of physically protecting my mother on the weekends and enduring bullying during the school week. Food was scarce at times because we depended, almost solely, on government assistance to eat.

Chapter 3
Stay the Course

God, teach me lessons for living so I can stay the course...
Guide me down the road of your commandments.
Psalm 119:33

Being on the honor roll at school was my only source of comfort and enjoyment. This made me feel important, as my report card became a source of pride for my mother, aunts, cousins, and sisters. I was in 7th grade when my grandfather became ill, and my family moved from the Mississippi Delta back to Hot Coffee. This move happened at a critical point in my life. I was beginning to get into trouble by hanging around the wrong crowd in the Mississippi Delta. Most of my friends and relatives, who I viewed to be role models in the Mississippi Delta, would later be sent to prison for drugs or murder. I am certain that if we had not moved back to Hot Coffee, this would have been my destiny as well. Though I later found Hot Coffee to be boring in comparison to my life in the Delta, at this juncture, I was glad to be moving. This move essentially saved my life.

Chapter 4
Attitude is Key

Attitude is more important than education, ability, reasoning, and facts. You decide which attitude to display daily.

After the Mississippi Delta, life back in Hot Coffee wasn't much easier. It was during this time that I met one of the most important leadership figures in my adolescent life. Uncle J C Fairley, who we affectionately refer to as Uncle J, was sixty-five years old and possessed a sixth grade education. Uncle J was my community's employer, banker, protector, spiritual advisor, and unequivocal leader. He was an entrepreneur and displayed compassion by hiring me to work in his watermelon field. Uncle J and I drove two hours to New Orleans, LA to sell the watermelons. Once in New Orleans, Uncle J had a two-pronged operation. We parked the one-ton truck at a busy intersection and sliced open a display watermelon. This enticed many people to stop and buy them. We then drove the pickup truck through the residential areas of New Orleans, and as my uncle would honk the horn, my cousins and I would be on the back of the truck screaming at the top of our lungs in our southern Mississippi dialect, "WE GOT YO MISSISSIPPI WAATAMELOONS!   RED TO DA RHYME!" Folks would come to the truck and ask, "How much dose watermelons?" and I would say, "Two dollas apiece," and they would say, "Nooo . . . too high" and I would reply, "Tell you wat, I'll give you two for fo dollas," and they would say, "We'll take 'em!"

Chapter 5
Wisdom is a Virtue

*By three methods we may learn wisdom: First, by reflection,
which is noblest; Second, by imitation, which is easiest; and
third by experience, which is the bitterest. Confucius*

I prided myself on being Uncle J's best
salesman and his favorite yeller in getting
prospective customers out of the house. Uncle
J frequently motivated me by saying, "Boy, you
know you can holla!" and "Keep bringing them out
of the house, Bob!" I learned so much from Uncle J
as he often taught about standards of conduct in a
raised tone and in his wonderful, southern
Mississippi dialect: "White folk'll help you if ya wuk
hard!" and "You may as well like'em (white folk) cuz
ya godda wuk for 'em." I will never forget when he
said, "Boy, if you go to jail for fightin, I'll gitchu out
cause I fought! If you go for jail for drankin, I'll

gitchu out cause I drank! But if you go to jail for stealin' or messing wit dat dope, you gon rot there!" I didn't realize it at the time, but Uncle J was shaping my work ethic, teaching the value of relationships, and explaining a zero tolerance policy for stealing and illegal drug use. His experience base was formed while growing up under the Jim Crow laws of the South but his declarations set a precedent in my heart.

Chapter 6
Embracing Change

For I know the plans I have for you, declares the LORD, "plans to prosper" you and not to harm you, plans to give you hope and a future. Jeremiah 29:11

I n the fall of my senior year of high school, I received a phone call from my girlfriend, informing me that I was going to be a father. I was only seventeen and the thought of raising a child was overwhelming. After a bit, I told my Spanish teacher, Mrs. Mayfield, and she asked her husband, the city Alderman, if I could work in their yard after school to help with the baby's expense. They took the time to develop a relationship with me and allowed me the opportunity to work for $3.35/hr (min. wage) to support my son. Mrs. Mayfield understood my immediate family issues and included me as part of their extended family. The Mayfield's were considered affluent, their children were educated, and they taught me responsibility, character, and the importance of education. I am still very close to this family today.

Chapter 7
Attitude Gives You Altitude

For the spirit God gave us does not make us timid, but gives us power, love and self-discipline.
2 Timothy 1:7
Attitudes are the little things that makes a big difference.

When my son, Robert Rashad Crosby, was born, I was determined to be a good father and a good provider, so I enlisted in the Navy in January of my senior year in high school. The first time I left Mississippi was when I left for Boot Camp in San Diego, CA. My recruiter had informed me that if I performed well, I could be promoted to E-2 when I left boot camp. I focused on this promise. Upon arrival, the Company Commanders gathered the hundred or so recruits and instructed each of us to sound off. Most of the recruits were shy and timid when called upon, but when it was my turn, I inhaled a healthy dose of God's fresh air and shouted at the top of my lungs, in my full southern Mississippi dialect:

"My name is Robert Crosby! Fo-two-seven- xx-xxxx! I'm from Hot Coffee, Mississippi! Favorite food is pinto beans and cornbread, Sur!" After my "sounding off" an eerie silence came over the group. The Company Commanders called me to the front and after quietly inquiring to ensure that I was in the right branch of service (Navy versus Marines) they gave me a spot promotion to Recruit Chief Petty Officer. They were compassionate leaders and I earned E-2 out of Boot Camp. I was very excited about becoming a Navy cook.

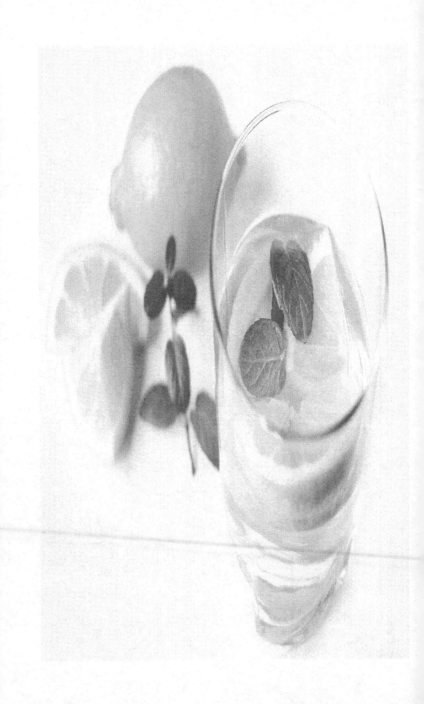

Chapter 8
Turning Lemons into Lemonade

Pace the crowd. Refuse to follow it.
Dare to Dream Big.

I reported to the USS Thorn in the winter of 1994 and was immediately assigned to the general mess to cook for a crew of about 350 people. I memorized the entire crews' first names so I could greet them by name as they came through my chow line. My chief noticed my initiative and persuaded me to go to the wardroom to cook for the officers. My shipmates sneered at that position and stated, "Rob, you are going to be a slave up there!" My buddies understood that in addition to cooking, the wardroom cook made the officers' beds, vacuumed their staterooms, washed their clothes, and cleaned their toilets. I forced myself to

29

love it because I viewed it as my only alternative and I wanted to be a squared away sailor. Also, I truly believed that the officers could not make good decisions if their stomachs were empty and if their accommodations were not properly maintained. In my mind, I was contributing to the mission of the ship by keeping them comfortable and well fed. One day, while vacuuming my Captain's stateroom closet, I saw his Service Dress Blues. After peeking out of the entrance to ensure no one was around, I tried on his jacket and cover. They both fit perfectly. I stared in the mirror for a couple of minutes and thought, "Maybe I can be a Naval officer?" I quickly replaced the uniform to its original position. A few days later, in the ship's library, I found a book entitled *Nimitz*. Reading about how Admiral Chester Nimitz, a poor boy from Fredericksburg, Texas, overcame challenges early in his career was very inspirational and gave me hope. I fell in love with this book. One day while reading, one of my shipmates snatched the book from me, looked at the cover with Admiral Nimitz's white face on the front, and said, "N(word) who do you think you are? You are a cook like us!" I laughed, but inside I felt like the little kid back in the Mississippi Delta all over again. The teasing by my shipmates intensified. I was labeled a kiss up and an "Uncle Tom." The isolation was horrible but my mind was freed in the evenings, as I would get lost in the book. Imagining that I was Admiral Nimitz became motivation for me to become an officer so I could lead my own ship someday.

Chapter 9
Facing Failures

My great concern is not whether you have failed but whether you are content with your failure.
Abraham Lincoln

I had begun to seriously consider becoming an officer, so I visited my Command Career Counselor and informed him of my aspirations. He told me about the Broadened Opportunity for Officer Selection and Training (BOOST) program, which was a college preparatory program designed to enable enlisted personnel to receive a commission in the Navy. I had to cross a major hurdle to get into the program, scoring a high qualifying mark on the SAT. Given my sparse academic background this would be challenging. I prepared for the SAT between standing watches and during breaks from feeding and taking care of the officers on my ship. Ensign Floyd, the only African-

American officer on my ship, noticed my efforts and committed himself to assisting me. Daily, after standing his watch, he would meet with me in the wardroom to go over the basics of algebra. Despite sometimes falling asleep in the middle of teaching a concept, he was committed to helping me achieve that passing score to get into the BOOST program. In spite of all of our hard work, my SAT scores did not qualify me for BOOST program. Still, I submitted my application and I was selected as an alternate, and later upgraded to a selectee. Upon acceptance to the program, I was introduced to calculus, trigonometry, and physics. These concepts were very foreign to me, but if selectees did not successfully graduate from the BOOST program, they would return to the fleet in their previous field. For me, going back to cooking and cleaning was not an option anymore. I studied continuously and graduated with distinction.

Chapter 10
You Are What You Think

The greatest discovery of our generation is that humans can alter their lives by altering the attitudes of their minds. As you think so shall you be.
William James

After graduating from BOOST, the Navy awarded me a Navy Reserve Officer Training Corps (NROTC) scholarship. I decided to choose a major that I could relate to cooking, so I chose chemical engineering. I related cooking to chemical engineering because I thought the subjects shared the same foundations such as maintaining an optimal pressure and temperature for a certain product, and regulating temperature and pressure at a microscopic level to yield a better product. I enjoyed my professors at Hampton

University as they went out of their way to help me achieve. I graduated Magna Cum Laude from Hampton University with a Bachelor of Science in Chemical Engineering.

Chapter 11
Sheer Effort

A pessimist sees the difficulty in every opportunity. An optimist sees the opportunity in every difficulty... Sheer effort enables those with nothing to surpass even the brightest that possess privilege and position.
Winston Churchill

After graduation, I was commissioned as an Ensign in the Navy. Once I passed the nuclear admissions test in Washington DC, the interviewing four-star Admiral stated, "Trade your spatulas in for some Nuclear Reactor Plant Manuals. Welcome to the Club!" The next stage was to complete Admiral Rickover's personally designed, academically rigorous, Nuclear Power School. Nothing at this point prepared me for the sheer volume of information I was required to understand and to be tested on weekly. I struggled. Several instructors worked outside their normal working hours to help me grasp concepts such as Reactor Theory and Radiological Controls. Eventually, I graduated from the school and was awarded the Director's Personal Excellence Award, an award given for maintaining a positive attitude and for logging the most study hours ever at the institution--almost 3000 hours over a six-month period. My family from Hot Coffee attended graduation and my mother and father cried audibly as I accepted the award. While hugging my mother as she continued to cry, she whispered in my ear in her warm and southern way, "I can't believe a person as smart as you came from an uneducated woman like me. Praise the Lord!" It was one of the proudest moments in my life.

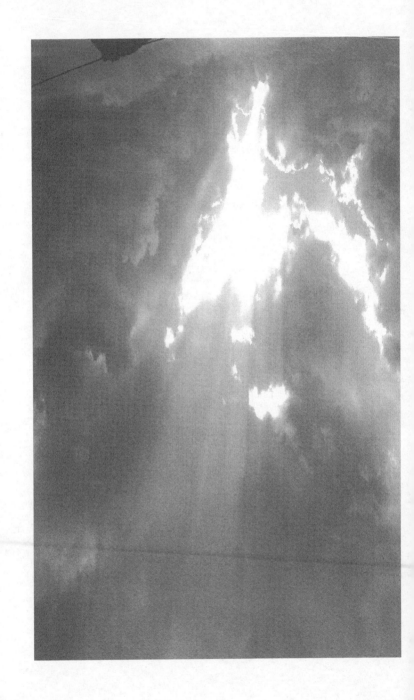

Chapter 12
Creating the "AWE" in You

A positive Attitude and a strong Work Ethic will inspire others to enable your success. You will be in AWE.
Robert Crosby

After finishing the Nuclear Power School training curriculum, I reported to my very first submarine. In the submarine community, training and education never cease. Within the first days of reporting, I was given a qualification card for Engineering Officer of the Watch (EOOW). I did well in grasping concepts on paper, but the practical applications of supervising and giving orders, especially in a casualty scenario, were very challenging for me. My immediate supervisor, the Engineering Officer, noticed that during the weekly Saturday night pizza celebrations among the officers in the wardroom, I was routinely absent. He would later walk through the engine room and find me behind a turbine generator practicing giving oral commands to members of the engineering spaces. From that point, he practiced with me daily until I achieved proficiency and qualified as EOOW. Additionally, my commanding officer took the time to ensure that I grasped certain concepts to qualify as Officer of the Deck. I would not be a submarine officer today, if it were not for the direct leadership of these two individuals.

Chapter 13
Helping Others

There is not self-made man. You will reach your goals only with the help of others.
George Shinn

After finishing my tour on the USS HAMPTON (SSN 767), the Navy sent me to the Naval Postgraduate School (NPS) to pursue an MBA in financial management. After graduation from NPS, I received orders to report to the ballistic missile submarine, USS RHODE ISLAND (SSBN 740), as the Weapons Officer. I was in charge of all of the ballistic missiles on board. After reporting, I soon developed too much of a "Gung Ho" attitude that adversely affected other members of the crew. Instead of publicly reprimanding me, the Commanding Officer and Executive Officer privately counseled me on the importance of understanding human relations and how my actions, albeit motivating, were contrary to the command climate on the submarine. The power of their example inspires me today.

Chapter 14
Missed Opportunities

We often miss opportunity because it's dressed in overalls and looks like work.
Thomas A. Edison

After leaving USS Rhode Island, I reported to Congressman Robert Brady's office as the Military Legislative Fellow. The Congressman's nomination numbers were extremely low and he was concerned about the apparent lack of interest students displayed for the service academies. The Congressman's district is comprised of a large underserved community; therefore, I saw an opportunity to make a difference in the lives of the children of the First District of Pennsylvania. I went to the district several times and spoke to many schools about my background and how the military afforded opportunities for me. The following year,

100 percent of the Congressman's nominations were filled - a first in Congressman Brady's 16 years in office. This would not have happened without the work place flexibility, which allowed me to share my story with youths of similar backgrounds.

Chapter 15
You are in Control

The longer I live, the more I realize the impact of attitude on life. Attitude to me is more important than facts. It is more important than the past, than education, than money, than circumstances, than failures, than successes, than what other people think or say or do. It is more important than appearance, giftedness, or skill. It will make or break a company... a church... a home. The remarkable thing is, we have a choice every day regarding the attitude we will embrace for that day. We cannot change our past... We cannot change the fact that people will act a certain way. We cannot change the inevitable. The only thing we can do is plan on the one thing we have, and that is our attitude... I am convinced that life is 10% what happens to me and 90% how I react to it. And so it is with you... We are in charge of our attitudes." ~ *Charles R. Swindoll*

Where I'm from, it's not uncommon for teen parents to live a life of which they are not proud. I'd like to believe that a major contributor to why so many people

57

went beyond the call of duty and reached out to help me is because they may have seen in me a bit of "A&W," attitude and work ethic. A child cannot choose their parents, their birthplace, academic ability, or social environment in which they are reared, but they can choose to have a good attitude and strong work ethic. Even as an adolescent, I had the ability to see the glimmer of hope in any situation and the ability to focus on doing my absolute best in any endeavor, whether it was achieving the honor roll in middle school or working on Capitol Hill. As I consider the future, I will look for A&W in my colleagues and subordinates so I can positively contribute to their lives as so many have contributed to mine. This life has been an amazing journey, my destination is uncertain, but I am enjoying this wonderful ride. My journey continues.

ABOUT THE AUTHOR
AND BOOST

Robert Crosby is a Lieutenant Commander and Nuclear Submariner in the United States Navy. Inspiring underserved youth and showing how the Navy can not only fight and win wars, but also can change lives, was the premise behind this book. Recalling his own experiences, Robert created B.O.O.S.T., Broadened Opportunity for Outstanding Student Selection and Tracking, a nonprofit organization that selects, tracks, and mentors youth in underserved areas to BOOST their possibilities by providing academic, leadership and character enrichment programs to ensure they too have the opportunity to reach their maximum potential. All proceeds of this book will be used to support BOOST, a 501(c)3 organization.

For additional information, please email BOOST at buildingboosters@gmail.com or go to www.boostachild.com.

Donations are tax deductible.